BAD PANDA

By Megan Gogerty

Bad Panda was first produced on October 13, 2012 by Iron Crow Theatre, Baltimore, MD, Steven J. Satta-Fleming, Artistic Director. The production was directed by Joseph W. Ritsch, with production design and stage management by Bryan Schlein, sets by Joseph W. Ritsch, costumes by Rebecca Eastman, lighting by Todd Mion and sound design by Joseph W. Ritsch.

The cast was as follows:

GWO GWO: David Brasington
MARION: Katie O. Solomon
CHESTER: Adam Cooley

ALL RIGHTS RESERVED
Original Works Publishing

CAUTION: Professionals and amateurs are hereby warned that this play is subject to royalty. It is fully protected by Original Works Publishing, and the copyright laws of the United States. All rights, including professional, amateur, motion pictures, recitation, lecturing, public reading, radio broadcasting, television, and the rights of translation into foreign languages are strictly reserved.

The performance rights to this play are controlled by Original Works Publishing and royalty arrangements and licenses must be secured well in advance of presentation. PLEASE NOTE that amateur royalty fees are set upon application in accordance with your producing circumstances. When applying for a royalty quotation and license please give us the number of performances intended, dates of production, your seating capacity and admission fee. Royalties are payable with negotiation from Original Works Publishing.

Royalty of the required amount must be paid whether the play is presented for charity or gain and whether or not admission is charged. Particular emphasis is laid on the question of amateur or professional readings, permission and terms for which must be secured from Original Works Publishing through direct contact.

Copying from this book in whole or in part is strictly forbidden by law, and the right of performance is not transferable.

Whenever the play is produced the following notice must appear on all programs, printing, and advertising for the play:
**"Produced by special arrangement with
Original Works Publishing.
www.originalworksonline.com"**
Due authorship credit must be given on all programs, printing and advertising for the play.

Bad Panda
© Megan Gogherty
Trade Edition, 2015
ISBN 978-1-63092-034-0

Also Available From
Original Works Publishing

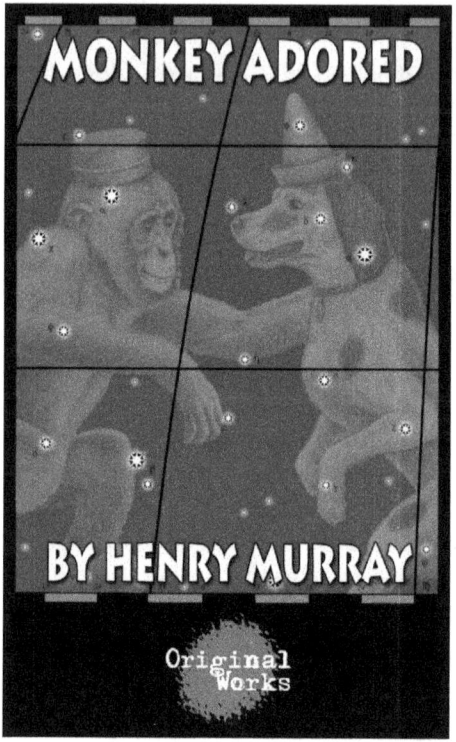

Monkey Adored by Henry Murray

Synopsis: What if animals evolved to the point where they could talk, sit in cafes and carry on interspecies love affairs? What if they decided to seek revenge on the humans who have subjugated them throughout history? A hybrid of ribald sex comedy and action/thriller MONKEY ADORED was lauded as a "Critic's Pick" by Backstage.

Cast Size: 4 Males, 2 Females

CHARACTERS
2M, 1 W

GWO GWO   (M)   A panda.
MARION   (W)   A panda.
CHESTER   (M)   A crocodile.

SETTING
An outdoor, free-roaming private animal reserve. It's a tranquil, lovely space. The set should be flexible, containing rocks and trees to climb on and to hide behind, and at different points suggesting these locales: a small decorative pond, a cave, and lots of bamboo.

COSTUMES
The wonderful thing about theatre is the animal characters don't have to look exactly like animals; it's enough to simply suggest their animal-ness. I encourage the designer to be creative. These characters are definitely animals, not humans, so they have to climb and move and feel very comfortable in whatever they're wearing and also not look exactly human when they do those things. And we should probably be able to see their faces. If I were producing this play tomorrow in my backyard with no money, I would put the actors in t-shirts that said "PANDA" and "CROCODILE," and let the audience fill in the details.

PAUSES AND PUNCTUATION
An ellipsis (…) means the speaker trails off. A sentence interrupted by an em-dash (–) means the speaker breaks off suddenly or is cut off by another. A pause is a longer ellipsis. A beat is a silence with a button on the end; a bounce. A shift is a new idea or tactic.

SCENE TITLES
I think it would be nice to display these at the beginning of each scene – projections, maybe, or placards on the side of the stage, or in some other surprising, delightful way.

BAD PANDA

ACT ONE

SCENE ONE: MARION AND GWO GWO EMBRACE THEIR NATURE

(Marion, a panda, is giving birth. Gwo Gwo, another panda, stands between her legs, ready to play catch.)

GWO GWO: Push! Push, Marion!

MARION: I'm pushing!

GWO GWO: You're pushing!

MARION: Do you see it? Is it coming?

GWO GWO: I see the head! I see the ears!

MARION: How many ears?

GWO GWO: Two! Two whole ones!

MARION: I'm still pushing!

GWO GWO: Here it comes! The body! It's enormous! It's a giant, it's a boulder, it's a log!

MARION: My baby!

GWO GWO: He's coming! He's coming!

MARION: It's a she!

GWO GWO: She's coming! She's coming! She's HERE!

(Marion collapses to the ground. Gwo Gwo holds up, not a baby, but a child's ball. He yells to the sky.)

GWO GWO (cont.): I am the proudest papa bear in the history of the world!

(Marion, from the ground, lifts her fists in victory to the sky.)

MARION: I am a mother! I am a mother!

(She sits up.)

GWO GWO: And then I take the baby and quick dunk it in the pond to wash off the juice.

MARION: Go! Go!

(He dunks the ball in a small, decorative pond several times.)

MARION (cont.): And I do my exercises!

(She does a series of quick calisthenics.)

GWO GWO: And then I bring the baby back to you and we both blow on it for several seconds.

(They huff and puff at the ball.)

GWO GWO (cont.): Then what?

MARION: Then…that's it. We get something to eat.

(They clap each other on the back.)

MARION (cont.): How's that?

GWO GWO: Really good. I think that was our best time ever.

MARION: You think so?

GWO GWO: Can you imagine? A baby? A new age! Glorious future!

(He holds the ball aloft, tenderly. Marion gets up and grabs it a little roughly out of his arms.)

MARION: Our baby will be the best baby of all the babies! Whoo!

(She throws the ball up into the air really high. It crashes to the ground, uncaught. Little pause.)

GWO GWO & MARION: *(Accidentally speaking at the same time.)* So.

(They laugh nervously. Little pause.)

MARION (cont.): We said we were going to practice all the parts.

GWO GWO: Yes, we did.

MARION: So should we? Practice?

GWO GWO: Oh. Um. Which part?

MARION: You know. The first part.

GWO GWO: *(Stalling.)* You look fat. You're gaining weight.

MARION: You sly thing! What a sweet thing to say.

GWO GWO: I can really tell in your face.

MARION: You should see my backside!

GWO GWO: Whoah! Shake that fat thing! You look wonderful. This place really agrees with you.

MARION: Does that mean you want to practice?

(Gwo Gwo stalls.)

MARION (cont.): We don't have to practice. We could talk it through some more.

GWO GWO: No, we should definitely practice. Mating season starts tomorrow, we want to be ready. No more talking. Time for action!

MARION: Okay!

GWO GWO: Great.

MARION: Good.

GWO GWO: Here I go.

MARION: All aboard.

(Pause. Nobody moves.)

GWO GWO: Maybe we should go through the reasons again.

MARION: Good idea.

GWO GWO: Reason one. We are the last two pandas on earth and we must propagate the species.

MARION: Reason two. You are a boy panda and I am a girl panda and boy and girl pandas are supposed to have babies.

GWO GWO: Reason three. Didn't we have a third reason?

MARION: Reason three. Because my mother did it, and her mother did it, and now I have to do it, whether I want to or not.

GWO GWO: Reason four. Because we must make more pandas. I think we're just restating reasons one and two. Reason five. Because we are good pandas.

MARION: Reason six. Because you want to have a baby with me.

(Little pause.)

MARION (cont.): Do you want to have a baby with me?

GWO GWO: The world needs babies… We must have a baby. This year. This season.

MARION: Okay then.

GWO GWO: Okay.

MARION: All aboard.

(Gwo Gwo screws his courage to the sticking place. He mounts Marion. He stands there. Marion waits expectantly. Minutes go by.)

MARION (cont.): Do something.

GWO GWO: I'm trying.

(More waiting.)

MARION: My back hurts. Do something.

GWO GWO: I'm trying, don't yell at me.

MARION: DO SOMETHING!

(Gwo Gwo lets out a roar of frustration and stumbles off away from Marion.)

GWO GWO: Stop yelling at me! My job is really hard! I have to concentrate, and you yelling, it gives me anxiety!

MARION: How do you think I feel? Standing there waiting for something to come flying at me! I thought you knew how to do this.

GWO GWO: How should I know? I've never mated before, at least not successfully or I don't think I have or if I have I didn't know I was doing it so how can I be held responsible? This is a lot of responsibility!

MARION: Don't get excited.

GWO GWO: And I can't do it when I get all jumbled!

MARION: You're right, I'm sorry. I shouldn't have yelled.

GWO GWO: You think I don't want to do it right? I'm trying! And I know I'm letting you down, not just you, but everyone. I'm letting everyone down right now! The whole species! It's too much pressure, Marion!

MARION: Okay. Let's take a breath.

GWO GWO: I just, I hate it. I hate being a panda!

(This pronouncement drops like a stone. Gwo Gwo immediately regrets it. Moments pass.)

GWO GWO (cont.): *(Quietly.)* I didn't mean that.

MARION: Oh. *(Pause.)* 'Cause I'm a panda.

GWO GWO: I know.

MARION: What's wrong with being a panda? *(Pause.)* I'm a great panda.

GWO GWO: You're the best panda in the world.

MARION: That's right. Way better than you.

GWO GWO: You're right. I'm sorry.

MARION: It's our first mating season. Now is not the time to panic.

GWO GWO: Don't be mad. I was just nervous. Put your head in my lap.

(She does. He curls around her.)

GWO GWO (cont.): We pandas have to stick together. That's our only chance.

(A log raises its head, revealing two eyes. It's not a log at all, but CHESTER, a crocodile. He is behind a rock and unseen by Marion and Gwo Gwo. He listens.)

MARION: Maybe we shouldn't bother.

GWO GWO: We have to. It's what nature intends.

MARION: You don't even like me.

GWO GWO: I like you very much, Marion.

MARION: Thank you. That's not what I meant.

GWO GWO: Don't be sad. You know what we forgot? Rituals.

MARION: Rituals?

GWO GWO: Mating rituals. That's why we're having trouble. We haven't done the right rituals to get us in the mood.

MARION: What are the rituals?

GWO GWO: I don't know. You'll have to make them up.

MARION: *(Flattered.)* Me?

GWO GWO: Of course you. You're going to be the mama bear. And anyway, you're the best at making up games, and rituals are like games.

MARION: Okay then. *(Beat.)* I like you, too, you know.

GWO GWO: Thank you.

MARION: Maybe we should take a break. Clear our heads. Think happy thoughts.

GWO GWO: I'll go exploring. And you can stay here and rest up for mating season. *(Beat.)* How long do you think we've been here? A few weeks? A month?

MARION: *(Shrugs.)* I'm glad you're my mate. I wouldn't want anyone else, even if.

GWO GWO: Even if.

SCENE TWO: ANOTHER ANIMAL

(Gwo Gwo is out exploring. He moves aside a clump of weeds. Behind it is Chester.)

GWO GWO: Oh!

(He takes a few steps back. Approaches again. Pushes the weeds back. Chester's still there, cool as a cucumber.)

GWO GWO (cont.): Hi. I didn't see you there.

(Chester moves out of the weeds. Doesn't take his eyes off Gwo Gwo.)

GWO GWO (cont.): Hi.

CHESTER: *(Draws out the word.)* Hi….

GWO GWO: You're not from the mountain.

CHESTER: Say again?

GWO GWO: The mountain. You never lived on the mountain. Did you?

CHESTER: I don't do mountains.

GWO GWO: What do you do?

CHESTER: Swamps.

GWO GWO: Ah. That's different from a mountain.

(Chester nods his head slowly.)

GWO GWO (cont.): I'm a panda bear. My name is Gwo Gwo. What's yours?

CHESTER: Chester.

GWO GWO: Nice to meet you. You're an alligator.

CHESTER: I'm not an alligator.

GWO GWO: Sorry.

CHESTER: Alligator, from the Spanish word, el Lagarto. Translation: The Lizard. Do I look like a lizard to you?

GWO GWO: So sorry.

CHESTER: I'm a crocodile. Alligator. *(Makes scoffing noise.)* Can an alligator do this?

(He darts to and fro in a crododile-ish fashion.)

GWO GWO: Maybe.

CHESTER: Wrong. They can't.

GWO GWO: Okay.

CHESTER: You wanna wrestle?

GWO GWO: Me? No. Pandas are nonviolent.

CHESTER: What a shame.

GWO GWO: Yeah…

CHESTER: Do I make you nervous?

GWO GWO: Yes.

CHESTER: Good. You should be nervous. I'm an apex predator. Know what that means?

GWO GWO: What?

CHESTER: I eat things. Animals. One day they're your friend, the next day they're my breakfast.

(Gwo Gwo giggles nervously.)

CHESTER (cont.): Don't believe me?

GWO GWO: Oh, I believe you.

CHESTER: Who's the other one?

GWO GWO: Who? Oh, Marion? That's Marion. That's my mate. Kind of. My new mate. This will be our first time. We weren't mates when we were on the mountain, but now we're here at this place, and she's the only girl panda and I'm the only boy panda, and all the other pandas… well. There are no other pandas. Anymore. We're the last ones. The only survivors. So we're going to mate. We decided. It should be interesting.

CHESTER: You a virgin?

GWO GWO: What? Oh. No. Yes, I mean. Have I ever mated before? No. This will be my first time. Both of our first times, actually. So no. Yes. First time.

CHESTER: How will you know if you're doing it right?

GWO GWO: We've been practicing.

CHESTER: With each other?

GWO GWO: Kind of. Talking it through, mostly.

CHESTER: Well, that's your problem right there. You can't talk and do it. You just gotta do it. You gotta... *(leans in close)* get wild.

(Gwo Gwo giggles again.)

CHESTER (cont.): You know where I live?

(Gwo Gwo shakes his head.)

CHESTER (cont.): What a shame. There's a cave east of here. Follow the river. Maybe you'll get lucky. You're interesting, panda bear. Most animals, they see me coming, they run away. Not you, though. What are you, stupid?

GWO GWO: A little.

CHESTER: Aren't you scared of me?

GWO GWO: A little. Not really. Maybe because I'm bigger than you.

CHESTER: Maybe. Maybe you think you can take me.

GWO GWO: Maybe.

CHESTER: Good luck with your mating season. Hope you figure out what goes where.

GWO GWO: Thanks. Do you know where we are? *(Beat.)* I don't know where we are. I was on the mountain. Then something bad happened. Now I'm here. One of my theories is maybe we didn't go anywhere, but maybe the mountain got up and left. But that doesn't make any sense. You don't know where the mountain is, do you?

CHESTER: There are no mountains. There're some dunes on the south end, but you're probably better off where they put you.

GWO GWO: They? Who's They?

CHESTER: Just…you know. The general They. The Royal They.

GWO GWO: The Royal They? What do They want? Are They bad?

CHESTER: Tell you what. You eat bamboo?

GWO GWO: Yes.

CHESTER: There's a lot of bamboo trees, where you live?

GWO GWO: Oh, yes. Lots.

CHESTER: Rip 'em up. Uproot 'em. Tramp 'em all down. Destroy them. See what happens.

GWO GWO: But that's our food! We'll starve!

(Chester shrugs.)

GWO GWO (cont.): Is there something wrong with it?

Chester: *(Laughs.)* Just see what happens. See ya, panda bear.

GWO GWO: See you later, allig– *(Off Chester's look.)* Crocodile.

(Chester exits. Gwo Gwo watches him go.)

SCENE THREE: MARION PREPARES; GWO GWO EXPERIMENTS

(Marion dances. Gwo Gwo watches her.)

MARION: So first I shake my bottom to the north. Then I shake my bottom to the south. Then I point to the moon with a dramatic gesture, like this. Then I make crooning noises, like this. Crooon! Crooon! Then I kiss the ground and make a snow angel.

GWO GWO: There's no snow.

MARION: Hmm. A dirt angel. That'll work, don't you think? And then, while I sit here and contemplate the shadow of the snow angel – dirt angel – you bring me all the bamboo you can carry. I have to eat and eat and eat. That way I'll stretch my stomach to make room for the baby.

GWO GWO: These are good rituals. What should I do next?

MARION: Oh, that part's easy. Imagine yourself mounting me. Over and over.

(Beat.)

GWO GWO: I met a crocodile... He seems like a very dangerous character. You should stay away from him.

MARION: That's okay. I'm not scared of any stinky ol' crocodile.

(Gwo Gwo gets up to inspect some bamboo trees.)

GWO GWO: This stuff tastes normal to you, right?

MARION: The bamboo? It's delicious.

GWO GWO: Huh.

(He starts yanking out some of the younger trees by the roots.)

MARION: Gwo Gwo! What are you doing?

GWO GWO: It's an experiment.

MARION: Well stop it! You want another famine?

(Pause. Gwo Gwo sits down. Another pause.)

GWO GWO: Did you know crocodiles live in swamps? This one doesn't. This one lives by the river. Can you imagine that? So many bugs and sticky things.

MARION: It sounds terrible.

GWO GWO: He challenged me to a fight.

MARION: Oh, no! You didn't, did you?

GWO GWO: No. I explained to him pandas were nonviolent.

MARION: Good work. You should stay away from the river, Gwo Gwo. Mother always said rivers are unsafe. And you shouldn't get in fights with crocodiles.

GWO GWO: No, you're right. That's very wise.

SCENE FOUR: GWO GWO EXPERIMENTS SOME MORE

(The river. Chester suns himself on a rock. Gwo Gwo enters.)

GWO GWO: Let's fight.

(Chester moves off the rock, contemplates him.)

GWO GWO (cont.): Come on. I'm serious. I can take you. I'm fast. I can climb things. I have these thumbs. I can do things with them. I'm bigger than you. I weigh more. I can take you. I ripped up some bamboo trees. Nothing's happened yet.

CHESTER: Just wait.

(Beat.)

GWO GWO: I used to fight all the time, you know. On the mountain. I had a boyhood friend. His name was Nan Nan. He's dead now. The Dark Day. It was a terrible catastrophe. All the pandas died. What's it like to be you?

CHESTER: Awesome.

GWO GWO: Have you ever mated before?

CHESTER: Oh, sure, love 'em and leave 'em. Apex predator. They tremble when I'm around.

GWO GWO: Is that true?

(Beat.)

GWO GWO (cont.): Are we going to fight, or what? I could take you. I'm not afraid of you. I'm strong. You don't scare me. I want to fight.

(Chester saunters over. Stretches out his finger. Traces a line down Gwo Gwo's belly.)

CHESTER: Okay. Let's fight.

(Neither of them move. An eternity. Then they spring at each other.)

SCENE FIVE: MATING SEASON BEGINS

(Gwo Gwo and Marion do it.)

MARION: Go! Go! Go! Go! Go! Go! Go!

(They collapse.)

MARION (cont.): Ooh. That's a good one. I think this one's a keeper. I can feel it. Little bits of you joining up with little bits of me. I'm all hot inside, did you feel it? I know this is going to be the time that makes my baby. I never wanted babies before, but I don't know. It seems like the right thing to do, right? We're doing the right thing. This is what pandas do. And when she gets here I won't be lonely anymore. Ooh! I wanna birth her right this second! You think it'll hurt? I don't think it'll hurt. Why would it hurt? Pain comes from bad things, not babies.

GWO GWO: You should rest.

MARION: What's wrong with your ear?

GWO GWO: I hurt it.

MARION: Is that a bite mark?

GWO GWO: It's nothing.

MARION: You wanna do it again?

GWO GWO: I thought you said that one was a keeper.

MARION: It's only the first day in our three-day window. Might as well be on the safe side. You know why they call it mating season, don'cha? 'Cause that's when we mate. Arr, matey! All aboard!

(She grabs him, tries to position him appropriately. It doesn't work.)

GWO GWO: I'm a little distracted.

MARION: Well, get un-distracted.

GWO GWO: How?

MARION: I don't know. Think about how much fun the baby will be, and how cute I'll look when I'm holding her. Here. Concentrate. Imagine. When I have my baby, I'm going to carry her on my back and feed her berries and bamboo. She'll roll around in the grass with me, and I will teach her all kinds of things. I'll tell her anything she wants to know, and I won't keep secrets. And even if she's a boy, I'll still love her. I'll grow her up to be a strong independent panda. And the two of us will be together, romping and tromping for the rest of our lives! Our problems will be over. All we need is a baby, Gwo Gwo. That is all we need.

SCENE SIX: MATING SEASON CONTINUES

(Gwo Gwo and Chester do it.)

GWO GWO: Go! Go! Go! Go! Go! Go! Go!

(They collapse post-coitus.)

CHESTER: Bad panda.

GWO GWO: Good crocodile.

CHESTER: It's my animal magnetism. You can't help yourself.

GWO GWO: You're incredible. I had no idea it could be this way. When Marion and I do it… Well. It's more cordial, for one thing.

CHESTER: I don't do cordial.

GWO GWO: Yeah, I know. You bit me.

CHESTER: What can I say? Top of the food chain, baby.

GWO GWO: Do you like girl crocodiles?

CHESTER: Females are weak. Always twittering around, whimpering, gazing wistfully at butterflies.

GWO GWO: Marion's not like that. Do you like Marion?

CHESTER: She's too grabby.

GWO GWO: Marion once punched me in the stomach. She meant it affectionately, but it really hurt. You don't like butterflies?

CHESTER: Well –

GWO GWO: I like butterflies. I'm not weak.

CHESTER: Everyone likes butterflies. I was making a broader point about…oh, never mind.

GWO GWO: You like me, though.

CHESTER: You pandas are something else.

GWO GWO: Does that mean you like me? I can't tell.

CHESTER: Do you like me?

GWO GWO: I think you're the coolest, strongest, most indestructible animal I have ever had the privilege to know.

CHESTER: Yeah, okay. I do then.

GWO GWO: Really? What do you like about me?

CHESTER: I don't know. I liked you since I first saw you. Weeks ago. I like the way you climb a tree. I like the way you curl up in a ball.

GWO GWO: We do that when we're scared.

CHESTER: And you're making a baby. That's… interesting. I'd never seen anyone like you two before. Pandas.

GWO GWO: I'd never seen anyone like you before, either.

CHESTER: How convenient.

(Beat.)

GWO GWO: We're both boys.

CHESTER: Astounding, your power of observation.

(Beat.)

GWO GWO: I feel very close to you. I feel I've been waiting my whole life for you.

CHESTER: Let's not get ahead of ourselves.

GWO GWO: Why wait? Don't you feel that way?

CHESTER: You pandas. You don't kid around.

GWO GWO: We're endangered. We don't have time.

(Chester reaches out and strokes Gwo Gwo's face.)

CHESTER: Yes. I feel that way.

(Gwo Gwo nods, sighs a big, yummy sigh.)

GWO GWO: Well, see ya. *(Gets up to go.)*

CHESTER: What? Where are you going?

GWO GWO: I've got to go. I shouldn't be here. I'm supposed to be making a baby right now.

CHESTER: Just like that? What happened to 'waiting your whole life'?

GWO GWO: I have to mate.

CHESTER: Just like that? Why'd you make me say all that stuff then?

GWO GWO: What do you mean?

CHESTER: Right. Good luck with the wife and kiddies, just leave the money on the dresser.

GWO GWO: What does that mean?

CHESTER: It means nothing, apparently. You gonna tell her about me?

GWO GWO: Of course not. It would only upset her. It's mating season. I shouldn't have distractions.

CHESTER: I see. A distraction.

GWO GWO: It's been good for her, I think, since we came here. She's really plumped out these past few weeks.

CHESTER: Well, la dee da. I'm a torpedo in the water, so la dee da for me.

GWO GWO: Are you mad? I have to go. It's not you, it's me.

CHESTER: *(Mocking.)* Oh, it's not you It's me. I've been going through some changes right now. I need some time, I need some space. I was just experimenting! Don't make me throw up.

GWO GWO: Are you mad?

CHESTER: Mad? I'm thrilled. You're doing me a favor, actually. I didn't know how to break it off without crushing you, you're so fragile and endangered.

GWO GWO: I'll be back in two days. I just have to go make this baby real quick.

(Beat.)

GWO GWO (cont.): You are mad. You don't seem to understand. It's mating season.

CHESTER: You've said that, like, a thousand times.

GWO GWO: Yeah, it's important. We're the last of our breed, Chester. If we don't do it, that's it. I need to concentrate. I don't see why you're taking this so personally. It was fun –

CHESTER: It wasn't fun. It was savage and blistering and bloodthirsty and wild. I ached from the back of my throat all the way down to my tail for you. I screamed for you. I bled for you. It was dangerous and upsetting and wild and mad. You domesticated animal. The one thing it never was is fun.

(Silence.)

GWO GWO: It'd be different if she already had a baby.

CHESTER: Then get her a baby already! I could do it if I wanted. How hard is it to get her a stupid baby?

GWO GWO: It's very hard, thank you very much!

(Chester snorts contemptuously.)

GWO GWO (cont.): What do you care anyway? You're an apex predator, love 'em and leave 'em.

CHESTER: I have feelings, you stupid dumb bear.

GWO GWO: I'm not really a bear, you know. You're the stupid one. Stupid.

CHESTER: Stupidity and crocodiles are mutually exclusive.

GWO GWO: Yeah, right. Crocodile. Cold-blooded predator. El Lagarto, reptilius, whatever.

CHESTER: Crocodylus. From the Greek "krokodeilos," meaning "pebble worm."

(Gwo Gwo laughs.)

GWO GWO: 'Pebble worm.' Ha!

CHESTER: I have a lineage that is over 240 million years old.

(Gwo Gwo laughs more.)

CHESTER (cont.): At least my kind knows how to survive!

(Gwo Gwo stops laughing, stung.)

GWO GWO: This was a mistake. *(Turns to go.)*

CHESTER: You wanna know who took you from the mountain? *(Beat.)* Sometimes They sneak up on an animal and then stab it. And They take it, and wrap it up in a sheet, and carry it to the Lab. You can see it from the far side of the river, if the water's high. And when animals go in there, they don't ever come out.

GWO GWO: How do you know this?

CHESTER: I'm smarter than you.

GWO GWO: So... They're not good, is what you're saying.

(Chester shrugs. Pause.)

GWO GWO: I'd better warn Marion. Don't be mad.

CHESTER: Ho, ho! Mad? Impossible. I give you this piece of information, this thing that you've been dying to know, and the first thing you think of is Marion. Mad? Mad? Why would I be mad?

GWO GWO: Wait. Does that mean you are mad? Or not mad? You have to admit, you are...cold-blooded. You can't take anything seriously.

CHESTER: My heart has four chambers! How many does yours have? I bet not as many as mine. I bet your heart just has one. And Marion's already in it. *(Beat.)* I sort of like you, you know. You think I'm a killer. *(Correction:)* Predator. There's a difference. I kill to live. And, okay, maybe I get some enjoyment out of it, but sue me, it's my nature. At least I don't go around sucking bamboo all day —

GWO GWO: Chester. My heart has two chambers.

(Gwo Gwo strokes Chester's snout. It's a genuine love moment. Chester reaches up and strokes Gwo Gwo's belly. Gwo Gwo picks up Chester in his arms. It's a powerful picture.)

(Marion enters, upset.)

GWO GWO (cont.): Marion? What are you doing here? How did you find me? Is everything okay?

MARION: I'm not pregnant. And you're a bad, bad panda.

SCENE SEVEN: CHESTER TAKES INITIATIVE

(Evening time at Chester's place. Marion sits dully, staring out. Gwo Gwo tries to comfort her.)

GWO GWO: Don't worry, Marion. We have two more days.

(No response from Marion.)

GWO GWO (cont.): It was my fault. I was doing it wrong, I wasn't following the plan. But I told him. I said, Marion's my mate, and we're going to have a baby no matter what. That's what I said. What is was, see, is he was giving me pointers. That's good, right? You'll see. Come tomorrow morning, I'll be on top of you before you know what hit you. Wholehearted. Okay, Marion? Okay?

(No response.)

GWO GWO (cont.): Listen. Marion. I found out something about this place. Remember the bad bug from the Dark Day, when all the pandas died? The bad bug that bites you and then you fall through the earth to the other side? That's part of it. It bites you – or stabs you, maybe. We need to be careful.

(Chester enters, with bamboo. He gives it to them.)

CHESTER: Here.

GWO GWO: Are you hungry, Marion? No? *(To Chester.)* Thanks anyway.

CHESTER: *(Softly, to Gwo Gwo.)* How does she know she's not pregnant? It's only been a day.

GWO GWO: She knows. A mother knows.

(Chester eyes Marion from afar.)

CHESTER: Stay here tonight.

GWO GWO: Chester. I have Marion with me.

CHESTER: So? You both stay here.

GWO GWO: Marion is not going to want to sleep in your slimy wet alligator cave. Excuse me, crocodile. *(Off Chester's look.)* What is it?

CHESTER: I don't think…it's a good idea…for her to be where she usually…can be found.

GWO GWO: What does that mean?

CHESTER: Oh, for pity's sake. Hide. Hide. I'm telling you to hide.

GWO GWO: Why? *(Beat. Recognition.)* The Royal They. You think They're going to stab her and drag her away in a sheet?

CHESTER: Your ability to detect nuance is staggering.

GWO GWO: What could They want with Marion? It's mating season. We're trying to make a baby.

CHESTER: Maybe They don't want her to make a baby.

GWO GWO: But we have to. If we don't make a baby panda, then... *(Beat.)* But that's cruel. How do you know this?

CHESTER: It's a hunch.

GWO GWO: What does that mean? Instinct? Crocodile instinct for danger –

CHESTER: I just know! I know them. The moss smells different when They're around. The birds stop singing when They've been by. I just know. Now for this plan to work, you gotta get out of here. It's too suspicious, both of you hanging around.

GWO GWO: Where should I go?

CHESTER: Get some rations. Stuff from the pond that will make her feel at home.

(Gwo Gwo springs into action.)

GWO GWO : Okay! Everybody just stay calm! Marion, I'm gonna go — I'm gonna go. I'm gonna get some things. I want you to stay here with Chester. Okay? Do you hear me? I'll be right back with your things, so just stay here! In the cave. Out of sight. Chester? Okay. We're gonna get through this.

(Gwo Gwo exits. Beat. Chester and Marion eye each other balefully.)

CHESTER: Good. We're alone. *(Saunters over to Marion.)* I understand you're in a bit of a pickle. Mating season, you can't conceive, your mate is clearly not interested in you. It's rough going for ol' Marion, isn't it?

MARION: What do you want?

CHESTER: Ah, ah! Wrong question. The question is not what does Chester want, the question is, what can Chester do for you?

(Marion sighs, like she has to do an unpleasant chore after a very long day, and stands. She wraps a paw around Chester's snout.)

CHESTER (CONT.): Hey!

MARION: Listen, reptile. I could kick your ass up and down this river. So let's get something straight. Gwo Gwo is my mate. Mine. He's the boy panda and I'm the girl panda and we are going to make a baby if it kills us. You seem like a real friendly crocodile. But pandas and crocodiles aren't supposed to be friendly, are they? It's unnatural. And you come in here, turning my mate's head when I am trying get him to focus. I don't appreciate it. It makes a hard job harder. So here's what you're going to do. You are going to back off. Disappear for a few days. Just until I get what I need out of that sorry excuse for a panda. And if you cross me on this score, don't doubt that I could kill you if I want.

CHESTER: Look, you're never gonna get a baby that way!

(She lets him go. He rubs his snout.)

MARION: What do you mean?

CHESTER: Ow.

MARION: What do you mean I'm never gonna get a baby that way?

CHESTER: You bruised my snout. You big bully.

MARION: Crocodile, you better –

CHESTER: The only way you're having a baby is if They let you.

MARION: They who? Who's They?

CHESTER: C'mon, Marion. You're not that dumb.

(Beat.)

MARION (cont.): Oh. *(Another beat.)* Oh. So I need Their permission? Their approval?

CHESTER: Something like that.

MARION: How do I do that?

CHESTER: Oh, you want my help all of a sudden? I thought you were going to kick my ass down the river. Which, by the way, you totally could not do. But sure, I could help you. If I wanted.

MARION: Why would you want to?

CHESTER: What an excellent question, Marion. I don't really. But let me put it to you this way. You want a baby. I want Gwo Gwo.

(Pause.)

MARION: We can deal.

CHESTER: See that? Common ground. That's called negotiation.

MARION: What do I have to do?

CHESTER: You know the west hill? Start walking. Climb that hill. About half way up, you'll start to feel sick inside. Your head will swim and your knees will get shaky. You'll be seized with a strong desire to turn around and go the other way. Ignore that feeling. Keep walking. When you reach the top of the hill…

MARION: What?

CHESTER: You'll have Their attention.

MARION: Then what?

CHESTER: Then nothing. State your case. See what happens.

MARION: Then I get a baby.

CHESTER: Then everybody gets what they want. Even Gwo Gwo.

MARION: You know a lot about this place.

CHESTER: Panda bear, I'm a crocodile. I've forgotten more than you'll ever know.

(Gwo Gwo enters, arms filled with bamboo and his toy ball.)

GWO GWO: Here I am! I've returned, safe and sound. What's going on?

MARION: We're getting to know one another.

GWO GWO: Oh. That's good. Is it good?

MARION: *(Turns to go.)* Good enough for me.

GWO GWO: Marion, where are you going? Don't go back to the pond, it's not safe.

MARION: You can't tell me what to do.

GWO GWO: But wait! Look, Marion. I got us some rations, and guess what I found floating in the pond. *(Holds up the ball.)*

MARION: Is it a baby?

GWO GWO: No.

MARION: Then who cares? *(She exits.)*

GWO GWO: *(To Chester)* What did you do?

CHESTER: Hey, she threatened me! I keep forgetting she's a bear.

GWO GWO: Not a real bear, a panda bear. It's - never mind. I'd better go after her.

CHESTER: Let her go.

GWO GWO: No, it's not safe. Sometimes They take an animal and stab it, you said.

CHESTER: Well.

GWO GWO: When I was at the pond. You know the bamboo trees I ripped up? Somebody planted some new ones. A whole bunch. Three months' worth of growth. Explain that.

(Chester opens his mouth to speak. Bang! The sound of a gun offstage.)

GWO GWO: Marion!

(He sprints off after the sound, Chester close behind.)

GWO GWO (cont.): Marion? Marion?

CHESTER: It's okay.

GWO GWO: What do you mean, it's okay? That sound. She could be hurt, she could be lying somewhere bleeding.

Chester: She's fine. They just took her.

GWO GWO: Oh, no, Marion. Why? She never did anything wrong to anybody! Why would they do that? What do they want? Maybe they tried to take her and she escaped -

CHESTER: She went to Them. She sought Them out. She wanted a baby.

GWO GWO: But that's crazy! She would never go to Them for a baby. Pandas make a baby during mating season, everybody knows that. *(Shift.)* What did you tell her?

CHESTER: Nothing.

GWO GWO: You said something to her. You told her to go to Them.

CHESTER: I just said, *(mumbles.)*

GWO GWO: Come again?

CHESTER: I told her, she's never going to make a baby that way.

GWO GWO: Through mating? What other way is there?

CHESTER: I don't know. Maybe They don't want you to mate. I mean, who knows what They want with you pandas? Sometimes the animals are sick when they get here. I didn't mention that before but it's true. Maybe Marion was sick, you don't know.

GWO GWO: She wasn't sick.

CHESTER: Well. I told her to...ask Their permission. *(Off Gwo Gwo's look.)* Hey, pal, you weren't giving her a baby, so I stepped up. I did you a favor. It's not like they're going to kill her. I mean, probably not.

GWO GWO: Ho, oh! Probably not! Probably!

CHESTER: I don't see what you're getting so mad about.

GWO GWO: You took my mate away! During mating season! What kind of cruel creature are you? My mate is lost, and you stand there...! That's cruel, Chester! I should've known. Crocodiles are known for their cruelty.

CHESTER: Actually, we're known for our tears.

GWO GWO: Oh, Marion. *(A wail.)* Marion!

CHESTER: So it's true. You like her better than me. Figures.

GWO GWO: You don't understand, you stupid animal. We're the only ones left. Don't you get it? It got very dark. The sky turned peculiar. And there was wind. Like the whole sky wanted to be someplace else. There was trembling. Of the ground. Of everything. There was a noise far away – a dark noise. And I ran. And the other animals, some of them were wild faces and some of them were frozen, dead. And then I couldn't run anymore, so I found a tree and started to climb. Because that's what you do, that's what my mother taught me, if there's danger on the ground and you can't run then you hide, find the tallest tree and climb far away. And that's when I felt the bite. The bad bug. I fell out of the tree. But I didn't hit the ground. I passed through it, deep into the earth, all the way down to the other side. And then I woke up. And everything was different. There was a pond and all the bamboo I could eat. All the others, they all died. Except for me. And Marion. And now she's gone. And I'm alone. And the worst thing that could happen has happened.

CHESTER: Oh.

GWO GWO: *(A sudden yell.)* I hate, hate, hate being a panda! I hate feeling this way, I hate losing everything! I'm running, I'm always running down the mountainside, I hate it, I hate it!

(Beat.)

CHESTER: It's not so bad at the Lab. She might like it. They check your teeth and poke you with things. And you sleep a lot.

GWO GWO: You said animals go to the Lab and they don't come back.

CHESTER: I lied. Sometimes they come back, but it takes a while. It depends on your teeth, I guess. I thought I was helping. Don't you see? Either They'll make a baby for her, which will take months, or They'll tell her, No baby for you, and send her back. Either way, you're off the hook. You're free!

GWO GWO: They can't make a baby for her. Only we can make a baby. Pandas.

CHESTER: You'd be surprised. They make a lot of crazy stuff.

GWO GWO: It wouldn't be a real panda.

CHESTER: Sure, it would. That's real bamboo, isn't it? They made that.

GWO GWO: They did?

CHESTER: It's delicious. Or so I've heard. Yuck.

GWO GWO: So… What am I supposed to do? Wait?

CHESTER: Now who's the stupid one? We're free! You can do what you like!

GWO GWO: She could be gone months, you said. I'm all alone. Pandas are supposed to mate. How can I be a good panda if I can't do that? If there's no girl panda... I'm nothing. You wouldn't understand.

CHESTER: No, I get it. You're alone. *(Beat.)* I think you're failing to see the opportunity here.

GWO GWO: What opportunity?

CHESTER: How do you know what a panda is, or does? Who says? Maybe a panda is an animal that tromps about in the sun all day and then takes a nap afterwards. I mean it. If you're the only panda, who's to tell you different? Think of something else to do.

GWO GWO: Like what?

CHESTER: Let me propose an alternative. You could be with me. All the time. We could be together. You know. Palling around and making trouble. And. You could watch me swim. Sometimes. You could...let me catch a fish for you. I could catch it in my jaws and then deposit it at your feet. And I could watch you climb a tree. And watch you move your thumbs around. I love your thumbs. And we could wrestle. And you could teach me things, and I could tell you about the things only reptiles know. I've been waiting my whole life for you. We could be like a family, the two of us. And we could be happy. Don't you think so? It's not so bad, is it? With me?

GWO GWO: So I could...do anything. I could be anything I want. I could be a crocodile?

CHESTER: Well. Sure you could. If you wanted. You'd be a great crocodile. We'd be two crocodiles, on the loose.

GWO GWO: I don't have to be a panda anymore if I don't want. Who's to tell me different? I bet it's fun to be a crocodile.

CHESTER: It's not all that exciting. But it's pretty exciting.

GWO GWO: I can do anything I want. I'm free.

CHESTER: Free. With me.

GWO GWO: But you lied to me. You tried to scare me. *(Beat.)* Let's stay at your place. I'm tired of the pond.

ACT TWO

SCENE ONE: GWO GWO GIVES HIS BALL AWAY

(Gwo Gwo and Chester, post-coitus. Gwo Gwo has a stupid grin he can't seem to lose. Both are deliriously happy.)

GWO GWO: Tell me again.

CHESTER: You don't wanna hear it.

GWO GWO: Yes, I do. You're floating in the water.

CHESTER: Yes.

GWO GWO: And the rabbit hops over and leans down to get a drink. Come on.

CHESTER: And the rabbit thinks I'm a log.

GWO GWO: Ha, ha, ha! Stupid rabbit!

CHESTER: And it lifts its nose up like it smells something, but then puts it back down towards the water.

GWO GWO: Then what?

CHESTER: Then I eat it.

GWO GWO: Snap! Outta nowhere! What else? Besides rabbit.

CHESTER: This morning?

GWO GWO: Ever.

CHESTER: Oh, I don't know. Turtle. Bird. Hyena.

GWO GWO: No way!

CHESTER: He had it coming.

GWO GWO: That is gross.

CHESTER: It's not gross.

GWO GWO: Yeah, it is.

CHESTER: You vegetarians are so pious.

GWO GWO: Hey, I ate a fish once.

CHESTER: Oooh, call the panda police!

GWO GWO: I caught it and ate it while it was still flopping around.

CHESTER: What did you think? Did you like it?

GWO Gwo: I like bamboo.

CHESTER: You're a doofus.

GWO GWO: No, you're a doofus.

CHESTER: No I'm not, I'm a rabbit.

GWO GWO: I eat rabbits for breakfast.

CHESTER: Help me, I'm a rabbit!

GWO GWO: I'm gonna snap you up! I'm gonna eat you!

CHESTER: Impossible, for I am an industrial strength rabbit!

GWO GWO: A what?

CHESTER: I'm a really big rabbit.

GWO GWO: Too bad for you, rabbit. I have a lineage over 240 million years old! I am a pebble worm!

CHESTER: No! Gasp! Not a pebble worm?! Whatever will I do?

GWO GWO: You will RUN!

CHESTER: Eeee!

(Gwo Gwo chases the "rabbit." He lands on top of him.)

GWO GWO: I've got you.

CHESTER: Ugh, you're killing me.

GWO GWO: I know!

CHESTER: No, you're crushing me! Get off!

(Gwo Gwo climbs off.)

GWO GWO: Stupid rabbit.

CHESTER: Okay, now you be the rabbit.

GWO GWO: No way. I am the crocodile.

CHESTER: I'm the crocodile.

GWO GWO: We can't both be the crocodile.

CHESTER: Okay. You be the crocodile, I'll be the panda.

GWO GWO: Oh, no.

CHESTER: Help! Help! I'm endangered! I eat bamboo and wash my face and curl up in a ball when I'm scared!

GWO GWO: I never should've told you that.

CHESTER: I'm scared all the time! All the live-long day! Won't you mate with me? Won't you give me love? Give me a baby!

GWO GWO: Okay, that's enough.

CHESTER: Gimme some kissy kissy luv-luv! I'm so cuddly, I'm so cute! I'm warm blooded all the time.

GWO GWO: I'm a crocodile. I smell like river water! I'm all bumpy and slimy! Everyone's afraid of me, I have no friends at all. I look like a piece of dead tree!

CHESTER: That's not true.

GWO GWO: Truth hurts, baby.

CHESTER: Okay, if I'm so horrible, and you're with me, what does that say about you?

GWO GWO: Terrible things. Horrible things.

CHESTER: So you're slumming?

GWO GWO: Slumming. Sliming. Rolling around in river muck.

CHESTER: Lucky you.

GWO Gwo: Lucky me.

CHESTER: I'm gonna bite you. Rabbit.

GWO GWO: Do it. Bite me.

(They wrestle. It's fabulous.)

(Marion enters.)

MARION: Hi there.

(They cease their wrestling.)

MARION (Cont.): Don't mind me. I'll just be a minute.

(Marion picks up Gwo Gwo's ball. The two are frozen mid-wrestle.)

MARION (Cont.): Pretend I was never here. *(Referencing the ball)* You don't mind if I take this, do you? You don't need it anymore, do you?

GWO GWO: Uh...

MARION: You don't mind if I give it to the baby?

(Silence. The word hangs in the air, like a cartoon ward balloon. Marion beams.)

GWO GWO: A baby?

CHESTER: Already?

MARION: Yeah, so if you don't mind, I have to get back. Can't leave her alone too long.

CHESTER: You have a baby?

GWO GWO: Is it - ? Is it mine?

MARION: It's a she. And she's mine. I wanted her, now I have her.

CHESTER: You left last night.

MARION: Yeah...

CHESTER: Just yesterday.

MARION: That's right.

CHESTER: And now you have a baby?

MARION: Lulu. After my mother.

CHESTER: Overnight? How did that happen?

GWO GWO: Chester!

CHESTER: How did it get here? Were you pregnant all along? Is Gwo Gwo the father? Is that somebody else's baby? Are there other pandas somewhere?

GWO GWO: Shut up, Chester!

CHESTER: It just seems amazing -

GWO GWO: You said they could do crazy things up there in the Lab.

CHESTER: Yeah, but -

GWO GWO: Well, They did it. They made us a baby.

MARION: Oh, no. They made me a baby. Me.

GWO GWO: You don't want me to be the panda daddy?

MARION: Fat chance.

GWO GWO: But, we had discussed -

MARION: That was before all... *(makes a gesture encompassing Chester and him.)* ...this. No thanks. You're a bad panda. I say that with love but it's true. The two of you are gross, no offense.

CHESTER: I'm not gross.

GWO GWO: I'm not gross, either.

MARION: Yes, you are. You are gross boys. Lulu and I will be fine on our own.

GWO GWO: Well, fine then. I don't want to be a panda anyway. I'm a crocodile now. Right, Chester?

CHESTER: You can't seriously raise a baby on your own.

MARION: What do you know about it, crusty?

(Chester sputters.)

MARION (cont.): That's what I thought. All talk. Just like that one. *(Points to Gwo Gwo.)* You think you're hot stuff, parading around this place, spying on us pandas - oh, I know about the spying - thinking you're all tough. You're not that tough. You're just a fickle-blooded lizard-brain who likes to sunbathe. You can't do anything real. Like have a baby, for instance. I'm the real apex whatever-thingy. So put that up your nose and blow it. Now if you'll excuse me, I've got a baby to raise. *(She smacks her own backside on the way out, in a "Kiss my asss"-type gesture. Exits.)*

GWO GWO: *(Calling after her.)* So I should just stay here then? Well, good! Fine! I'm going to do crocodile things which you wouldn't understand because they're vicious and nasty! Right, Chester? Right?

CHESTER: "Crusty?" Crusty?!

GWO GWO: Yeah, that was a low blow.

CHESTER: The nerve of that panda. Where does she get off - ?

GWO GWO: She can be mean sometimes. Hey, let's play a game.

CHESTER: I can do real things. I can do plenty of real things.

GWO GWO: Sure, you can.

CHESTER: She saunters in here like she owns the place. This is my place! So she can, what? Rub it in our faces that she has a baby now? Who cares? Who'd want a stupid dumb baby?

GWO GWO: Babies are nice.

CHESTER: Ha! Nice? Babies? That's rich.

GWO GWO: They are. They're warm and soft and smell nice. Haven't you ever seen a baby?

CHESTER: Of course I've seen a baby. I mean... I was a baby. And I did not smell nice.

GWO GWO: Well, don't worry about it. Here's what I think we should do. There's a hollow log that I happen to know has a squirrel living in it. Let's pitch rocks at it until he comes out and scolds us. Won't that be fun? And then we can say, "What are you going to do about it, squirrel?" And he'll be so flummoxed he'll go right back inside. What do you think?

CHESTER: And another thing. Lulu? That's a dumb name for a baby. If I had a baby, I'd name it something like Kill Face.

GWO GWO: I've never heard of a baby named Kill Face.

CHESTER: Believe me, it's a much better name. Baby. You know what I think? She didn't have a baby.

GWO GWO: Of course she did.

CHESTER: No, she didn't. She's just saying that.

GWO GWO: Why would Marion say something that wasn't true?

(Chester sputters.)

GWO GWO (cont.): You're getting upset. This is a good thing. She has her baby now, everyone's happy.

CHESTER: But she said I was a ...!

GWO GWO: That's Marion for you. Don't get me wrong, I like Marion very much, but between you and me, she can be a bit tough to take.

CHESTER: But what if - ?

GWO GWO: I don't like to argue with Marion. We just end up saying hurtful things. Mostly her. If she says it's her baby, then it's her baby. It's good. My job's done. Species saved.

(He practices his crocodile-ness.)

CHESTER: If she had a baby, why didn't she bring it with her? Why isn't she with it all the time?

GWO GWO: I don't know. Maybe she put it up a tree for safekeeping.

CHESTER: She says to me, she says, "What do you know about it, crocodile?" I'll tell you one thing I know. I know you shouldn't leave a baby up a tree!

GWO GWO: Let's do something else. I saw a bird's nest in a tree. Let's shake the tree and guess how many birds fall out. I guess three.

CHESTER: And another thing. I don't sunbathe.

GWO GWO: Yes, you do.

CHESTER: For medical reasons only! For my blood. You know, I have feelings.

GWO GWO: I know. You keep talking and talking about them.

CHESTER: I want to see it. The baby.

GWO GWO: No.

CHESTER: If she's got a baby, then let me see it.

GWO GWO: She said she doesn't want us around. She was very clear.

CHESTER: Oh, so she can just waltz in here, la dee da, I have a baby, and then nothing?

GWO GWO: Yes.

CHESTER: Screw that noise. I'm taking a look.

GWO GWO: No. *(Grabs Chester, immobilizes him.)*

CHESTER: Let me go.

GWO GWO: No.

CHESTER: Let me go!

GWO GWO: No. We're not seeing the baby.

CHESTER: Just a look. One look. One quick look real fast.

GWO GWO: It's not your baby. She doesn't want us, we don't want her. Fine. Can't you just be a crocodile with me? Please? We were having so much fun before. We can wrestle. We can make some trouble. You can bite me. Let's be crocodiles. Forget babies. You know what crocodiles do with babies?

CHESTER: What?

GWO GWO: Nothing. So let's do that.

SCENE TWO: NEW ALLIANCES

(Marion and the baby, alone.)

MARION: Well, here we are! That's the pond. Again. And that's some bamboo. What a lovely walk. What would you like to do today? We could go swimming. Well, no. I guess you can't go swimming, can you? We could climb a tr- No. We could...sit here. Some more.

(Pause.)

MARION (cont.): What do you want? Just tell me. Just tell me. Anything you want.

(Pause.)

MARION (cont.): Be. Interesting.

(Pause. She sighs.)

MARION (cont.): You're very cute, I'll give you that. You just are so... *(Surprisingly hostile about it:)* cute. *(She stares wistfully off.)* Did you know your mother has the all-time record for breath-holding under water? Not just of the pandas. Of all the animals. Except the fish, but they cheat. That's right. All-Time Record. Do you know how I got that? Practice, baby. Hard work. It's not like I woke up with these lungs. And now. I haven't been in the water in ages. Not that I'm blaming you. It's not your fault you're keeping me from reaching my potential. I just want you to know the sacrifices. I want you to appreciate all I do for you. Or don't do. For you. Because you're so, so cute. What's that? You want to see me dance around? You got it.

(She does an impressive dance.) Hey. No sleeping. Pay attention to this dance. Fine, then. My mother used to love to watch me dance. I would dance for her all the time. Stupid Dark Day.

(Gwo Gwo and Chester enter.)

GWO GWO: Hello, Marion.

MARION: *(Brightening.)* Oh! Hello! Hi there! Look who it is. Visitors. Hello.

GWO GWO: Don't be mad.

MARION: Why would I be mad?

GWO GWO: You told us to leave you alone.

MARION: Oh. Well. Just this once. What are you doing here?

CHESTER: Gwo Gwo wants to see the baby. *(Shoves him forward.)*

GWO GWO: No, I don't!

CHESTER: Yes, you do.

GWO GWO: No, I don't!

MARION: You want to meet the baby? I'll show you. But no touching.

(She shows them the baby.)

GWO GWO: *(To Chester.)* See? I told you.

CHESTER: What does it do all day?

MARION: Oh, all kinds of things. Lots of things. She's so cute! I bring her bamboo. Which she's not that interested in yet, she doesn't have any teeth. I put her in her bed. I take her out of her bed. I take her to and from the tree. I talk to her. At her. Our days are just so full. I think about before she came, I don't know what I did with my time then. Really, what did I do all day? I used to swing on branches, really high ones. Of course, now. Well. No branch swinging. Too dangerous. It would be, you know, not good. And we can't not be good, you know. We must be good. This is my job now and I love it. Love love love love love it. Really.

GWO GWO: Sounds boring.

MARION: Well, that shows what you know.

GWO GWO: Chester and I play games all day. We wrestle and bite each other. He's going to teach me to kill a rabbit, but he says I'm not ready for that yet.

MARION: Sounds dangerous.

GWO GWO: Oh, it is. And you know what else? I like it. Chester teaches me all kinds of things. He's bad.

(Chester has been staring at the baby. Marion notices.)

MARION: Oh, yeah. Real bad. *(To Chester.)* Shake your head, your eyes are stuck.

GWO GWO: Chester didn't think you had a baby.

MARION: Well. I did.

GWO GWO: *(To Chester.)* Satisfied?

CHESTER: Where's the eggshell?

GWO GWO: What?

CHESTER: I thought they...came in a shell.

GWO GWO: Like a turtle shell?

MARION: No shell. Just baby.

CHESTER: It's...furry.

MARION: *(Laughs.)* It's a panda. What? What's your problem?

CHESTER: Nothing.

MARION: No, say it.

GWO GWO: Let's not.

MARION: No, you've got something to say. You wanna tell me off? You wanna fight me? Here's your chance. You came out all this way. Just say it.

(Beat. The pandas look at Chester expectantly. He bursts.)

CHESTER: Lulu is a dumb name for a baby!

(Beat.)

MARION: My mother's name was Lulu.

CHESTER: Well, your mother had a dumb name. What if she gets lost? You'd have to go through the woods yelling, "Lulu! Lulu!" Number one, it's not a sound that carries so you're already in trouble there. Two, it's a defenseless name and it tells all the predators that the lost baby is easy prey, and three, if it were up to me, if someone were calling for me, "Lulu! Lulu!" I'd be too embarrassed to answer. It's a stupid, stupid name, and frankly, it's irresponsible.

GWO GWO: You've put a lot of thought into this.

(Beat.)

MARION: You like this baby.

CHESTER: No, I don't.

MARION: You wanna hold her?

CHESTER: *(Quickly.)* No.

MARION: Just a little bit.

CHESTER: No, thank you.

MARION: What's the matter, you scared?

CHESTER: Yeah, right. Me? Scared of that? It looks diseased.

GWO GWO: It's not diseased.

CHESTER: Well, keep it away from me is all I'm saying.

MARION: I think you want to hold this baby.

CHESTER: What? No. Gross.

MARION: I think you do.

GWO GWO: No, he doesn't.

CHESTER: No, I don't. I wanna eat it. I eat animals and you should all be afraid of me.

(Marion and Gwo Gwo exchange a look.)

MARION: C'mon. Hold her.

CHESTER: Look. I'm a crocodile. I do two things: wait, and attack. Stalk and kill, that's it. I don't hold babies.

MARION: You could hold this one.

CHESTER: No!

MARION: We won't tell anybody.

CHESTER: Tell the world, I'm not touching that thing! I could eat it in one snap.

MARION: Yeah, but you won't.

CHESTER: I could, though.

MARION: But you won't. You're a nice crocodile.

CHESTER: No, I'm not. Take that back!

GWO GWO: Better not antagonize him, Marion. It's not wise.

MARION: *(She holds out the baby like a puppet.)* "Hello, Chester! My name is Lulu!"

CHESTER: Stop it.

MARION: "Won't you give me a hug? Won't you give me some loving kisses?"

CHESTER: What's the matter with you? I am a crocodile! I have sharp teeth and...scales! Where is your dignity? *(Marion waits patiently.)* Oh, for pity's sake. Fine.

(Marion holds out the baby in front of Chester. He takes it, as if he expects it to turn into a scorpion.)

GWO GWO: Um…

MARION: Now say coochie coo baby.

CHESTER: You're a lunatic if you think that's happening.

MARION: Just one coochie coo. Please.

CHESTER: I'm not speaking in a funny voice. You can forget that.

MARION: Use your normal voice. Your normal voice is a tinkling melody.

GWO GWO: I don't know if this is a good idea.

MARION: Ssh.

CHESTER: *(Halfheartedly.)* Coochie coo... Coochie coo, baby. *(He snuggles the baby closer to himself.) (For real this time.)* Coochie coo... He's so warm.

MARION: It's a she.

CHESTER: She's so soft and warm.

MARION: Uh, huh.

CHESTER: *(To the baby)* Hi, there! Hi, little panda! Hi! It's your Uncle Chester. I mean, Chester your... neighbor. Your friend. Your dad's... *(To Marion, slightly panicky.)* What do I do?

MARION: It's okay. She likes you.

CHESTER: She does?

GWO GWO: She does?

MARION: Sure. See that expression on her face? That means she likes you.

CHESTER: She likes me. Neat.

GWO GWO: Okay, that's enough.

MARION: Maybe you and Gwo Gwo could take her for a few days.

CHESTER: What?

GWO GWO: What? No. No, no, no. This is a very bad idea. Marion, think. You want to entrust your baby, your cute, precious baby, to a couple of nasty, blood-thirsty crocodiles?

MARION: Oh, pshaw. He's not so nasty. Look at him.

GWO GWO: Chester, be nasty for Marion. Say something really mean. Tell her she's a stupid bear and, and, and she smells bad. Go on, tell her. This is a bad idea.

MARION: *(To Chester.)* Maybe we could watch her together, just until you get the hang of it.

CHESTER: *(Looks at the baby.)* I can't believe you would ask me such a thing.

MARION: Why not? You seem very interested in us pandas. And you know things. Helpful things. And I don't know, you might want a soft thing to hold sometimes.

GWO GWO: Marion, let's think this through. Chester is a crocodile, and crocodiles have very different priorities than pandas. Right, Chester? Right?

CHESTER: Coochie coo, baby. She looks like you. *(Chester regards Marion.)* She's beautiful.

(Marion smiles like a new day dawning.)

SCENE THREE: LIBERATION

(Chester and Marion sit on the ground. They play an elaborate patty-cake game. They are having a total blast.)

(Sitting on a rock to the side is a large television. The animals pay it no mind.)

CHESTER AND MARION: Betty was a beaver, Betty was a bear
Betty met a bunny and she bit it on a dare
One two seven five, twenty-three skiddoo
Skippity up, skippity up, skippity up, peanut!
My mama said your mama was
Feather feather, frank frank
Feather feather, fin
Feather feather in the weather
Feather in the bin
Two four seven eight
Wocka chicka wocka chicka
FREEZE!

(They freeze.)

(Gwo Gwo enters, sees them frozen, and stalks off.)

CHESTER: You moved!

MARION: No, you moved!

CHESTER: Cheater!

(Marion laughs and rolls around.)

CHESTER (cont.): Okay, okay, okay. Even faster.

MARION: Okay.

CHESTER AND MARION: Betty was a beaver, Betty was a bear
Betty met a bunny and she bit it on a dare
One two seven five, twenty-three skiddoo
Skippity up, skippity up, skippity up, peanut!...

(Gwo Gwo enters again, all huffy.)

GWO GWO: Excuse me!

(They stop their game.)

GWO GWO (cont.): I am trying to hunt. I need silence.

MARION: Hunt? What are you hunting for?

GWO GWO: Dangerous prey. For my dinner. You wouldn't understand.

MARION: Ooh! Dangerous, scary, terrifying bamboo! Wa-a-ah!

(She shakes a bamboo tree at Gwo Gwo. Chester laughs. Gwo Gwo shoots him a look. Chester shuts up.)

GWO GWO: Very funny. Shouldn't you be mothering the baby or something?

MARION: Shows what you know. The baby is asleep.

GWO GWO: Alone? Unguarded? What about predators?

MARION: What predators? You?

GWO GWO: How about snakes. Leopards. Crawling things!

CHESTER: I'll get her. She likes it when I wake her up.

(Chester exits. Gwo Gwo glares at Marion.)

MARION: What?

GWO GWO: You know what.

MARION: They don't have leopards here. Just friendly animals like Chester.

(Chester enters with the baby.)

CHESTER: Here she is!

GWO GWO: This morning, I ripped up some clover. Some rabbits were eating it, but I didn't care. I just ripped it right up. And then I... I urinated. Right in the middle of the field. All these animals were watching, but I didn't care. I. Just. Kept. Urinating.

CHESTER: Are you hungry, little girlie? Do you got a rumble in your tumble?

MARION: Here, gimmee. *(Chester hands Marion the baby. Marion gives her a little toss in the air.)* Who's my girl? Who's my little girl? Whoo! Whoo! *(Her tosses grow ever higher.)* Whoooo!

GWO GWO: Marion! Be careful!

MARION: Oh, she's fine. She likes it. Whooo!

GWO GWO: You're going to drop her.

MARION: Am not.

GWO GWO: That's not how you take care of a baby. *(Takes the baby.)*

MARION: How would you know?

GWO GWO: You need to be more careful.

MARION: Don't tell me how to mother.

CHESTER: Here, I'll take her. She likes it when I carry her.

(Chester tries to take the baby. Gwo Gwo doesn't notice. He inadvertently moves out of his way.)

GWO GWO: Just because you gave birth doesn't mean you know what's best.

MARION: Yes it does. You can't tell me what to do.

CHESTER: Here, I'll just – *(He tries for the baby again. No soap.)*

GWO GWO: You leave her in the cave for hours at a time –

MARION: Nuh, uh!

GWO GWO: – so you can go gallivanting off for play-time –

CHESTER: All this yelling, I don't think she likes it, she just woke up –

GWO GWO: You're a bad mother!

MARION: That's rich, coming from you. Always wandering around, stalking things. Always playing at being tough. What about my needs? What about Marion's fun times?

CHESTER: Why don't I take Lulu on a walk?

MARION: *(Snatches the baby from Gwo Gwo.)* Am I always supposed to come in second to this baby? Is that the way it is? Well, forget that. It's Marion's turn now, isn't it, Lulu?

GWO GWO: Lulu thinks you're a bad mother!

MARION: Lulu hates you! Lulu thinks you're a bad panda. I'm a wonderful mother. Aren't I, Chester?

(They turn to look at Chester. He makes faces at the baby in Marion's arms.)

CHESTER: Coochie coo, baby...

GWO GWO: Chester, will you leave the baby alone? Where is your dignity? For pity's sake.

MARION: Leave him alone.

GWO GWO: If you act like a mother and he acts like a crocodile, everything will be fine. Come on, Chester. Let's go intimidate some rodents.

CHESTER: I like playing with the baby.

GWO GWO: It's not your baby.

CHESTER: It's as much my baby as anybody's.

MARION: That's right.

GWO GWO: She's a panda baby.

CHESTER: So? I feed her and rock her and put her to bed. That makes her mine. *(He takes the baby.)* I never knew my father. In my family, the mother lays her eggs along the riverbank, and the father swims over, thinks some happy thoughts and swims away. No 'let me teach you how to fish, son' or 'let me show you how to sunbathe.' Not even a 'Good luck, kid, hope you make it to adulthood.' We're on our own in this world from day one. I've always wanted to have something to love and take care of. Is that so wrong?

MARION: That's beautiful.

CHESTER: I love this panda baby! And if loving pandas is wrong, I don't want to be right.

GWO GWO: Oh, gross. You sound like a panda.

CHESTER: So? Maybe I want to be a panda.

GWO GWO: You can't just call yourself a panda and then be one.

CHESTER: You call yourself a crocodile.

(Beat. Gwo Gwo is visibly stung.)

MARION: Ooooooh! Busted!

CHESTER: I didn't mean –

MARION: Fight! Fight!

CHESTER: Marion, would you knock it off, please?

MARION: You can't tell me what to do.

CHESTER: Just – Go get Gwo Gwo's ball. It's in the clearing.

MARION: Why would I want his stupid ball - ?

CHESTER: Marion. Please. Go get the ball.

MARION: Fine. I'm not taking the baby.

CHESTER: Fine.

MARION: Fine. *(She exits regally.)*

CHESTER: I'm sorry. I shouldn't have said that. You're a great crocodile.

GWO GWO: Do you even like me?

CHESTER: What?

GWO GWO: Or were you just using me to get to Marion and the baby?

CHESTER: Of course I like you. I liked you from the moment I saw you.

GWO GWO: No, you don't.

CHESTER: I do.

GWO GWO: How do I know you're not lying to me?

CHESTER: *(At a loss.)* I'm...not.

GWO GWO: What do you like about me?

CHESTER: Everything. I like how soft you are. How warm. How endangered.

GWO GWO: Those are all the things I hate about myself. How can you like those things? I'm scared all the time, Chester. Do you know how exhausting that is? Maybe we pandas are supposed to go extinct. Maybe we weren't built to survive.

CHESTER: I like pandas.

GWO GWO: How come we don't wrestle anymore?

CHESTER: Is that all? We can wrestle. Let's wrestle. I'll take you right now.

GWO GWO: I want you to want to wrestle with me!

CHESTER: Gwo Gwo, look. It's very tiring being a parent. I'm up all night long with the baby...

GWO GWO: Oh, forget it. What happened to you? Baby worshipping, patty-cake-playing you. Look at you, Chester. You're supposed to be strong. You're supposed to be vicious! Fast! Indestructible! You're not supposed to lollygag around and play daddy with a panda girl! You're a crocodile! You're a wild animal.

CHESTER: Yeah.

GWO GWO: You're a predator. You have a lineage. You eat things!

CHESTER: So?

GWO GWO: So! You're supposed to be the opposite of me!

(Beat.)

CHESTER: You don't understand me at all. Not from day one. What do you think I am? Do you think I...? I'm not going to be your mid-life crisis. I'm not a fantasy figure that will take you away from all this.

GWO GWO: But you're a wild animal, Chester! You're supposed to want to be wild!

CHESTER: I'm not wild. I was born right here.

GWO GWO: What?

CHESTER: Domesticated. And I've never eaten a hyena, and I've never killed a rabbit. I wanted you to think I was cool.

GWO GWO: Domesticated?

CHESTER: *(Shrugs.)* They raised me from a hatchling. Gave me food. Let me wander around. They used to try and keep me away from the other animals. There was this koala one time. He had two broken legs. And he was real afraid of me. I just wanted to... I was just curious. Anyway. They don't stop me anymore. I guess They just lost interest. Anyway, They know I'm not going to hurt anybody.

GWO GWO: Why not?

CHESTER: I'm a vegetarian. *(Beat.)* And then you. I never met anybody like you before. The other animals – they come in sick, right? And then they die and They come in and take them away. Or else they come in sick, and then they get better, and They come in and take them away. They never bring in two. But there are two of you! And you're so warm and soft. And the way that you curl around each other and protect each other! And you talk like there's only two of you, but two seems like a lot. Two is a big number! If there's two of you, you can never be alone. I want you to curl around me like that. I want to be a panda, too.

(Marion enters with the ball.)

MARION: And another thing! Boys are stupid. The problem with this place is, there's too many boys!

GWO GWO: For pity's sake, Marion, leave us alone. We're in the middle of something here.

MARION: Oooh, a lover's spat? Gag me with a stick. You're such a bad panda, Gwo Gwo.

GWO GWO: That's it. I'm a bad panda? I'm a bad panda?

CHESTER: Okay. Let's calm down…

GWO GWO: Marion. You pick up that baby.

MARION: No.

GWO GWO: You pick up that baby and cuddle it!

MARION: No!

GWO GWO: I swear to the heavens, Marion, you pick up that baby or else –

MARION: Or else what? What are you gonna do about it?

CHESTER: *(Picks up the baby.)* Okay, I've got the baby. Look. See? It's fine. I've got it. Coochie coo, baby. Everything's fine.

MARION: I hate that baby!

GWO GWO: *(Gasps.)* Marion!

MARION: There, I said it. It's awful, terrible, what's wrong with me, I know it, but it's true! I hate that baby! HATE. I thought it would be exciting, being a mother. Full of teachable moments and happy explorations. But instead it's really boring. Hold the baby. Feed the baby. Watch the baby. Don't drop the baby. Don't take the baby up the tree! Don't drown the baby! It makes me sick!

GWO GWO: Stop it! Stop saying that right now!

MARION: But it feels so good to say it out loud! It feels so naughty and right! *(Yelling.)* I hate that baby!

GWO GWO: Shut up, Marion!

MARION: What a rush! There's something terribly wrong with me, I think. How is it that it makes me feel better?

CHESTER: You're just having a bad day, is all. Your maternal instincts are on the fritz.

MARION: I don't have any maternal instincts. Ha! Not a one! Zero! I have plenty of instincts, but my instincts say things like, 'Go play, Marion! Go swat at some bees!' You know. Fun things.

CHESTER: I fail to see how bee swatting compares to this baby.

GWO GWO: You see that? Even Chester agrees! You're a bad panda, Marion. Even Chester's a better mother than you.

MARION: Fine! Let Chester do it! I don't want to be the mother anymore. The mother job stinks! Chester, you can be the mother from now on.

CHESTER: Well.

MARION: In fact... *(A sudden inspiration.)* Be my mother.

CHESTER: What?

GWO GWO: What?

MARION: No, really. Be my mother, Chester. Praise me when I'm good, and when I'm bad, spank me.

CHESTER: Uh...Let's not get ahead of ourselves.

MARION: That's what I need, I need somebody strong. Somebody in charge. My mother was a real bear. She'd spank me and I'd feel it for weeks. Spank me, Chester! Spank me!

CHESTER: Stop it! Get a hold of yourself!

MARION: I don't want to get a hold of myself, I want you to get a hold of me! I'm tired of being the responsible one, the one who follows all the rules! I'm a bad, bad girl and I need to be punished!

GWO GWO: Stop it, stop it, stop it! You've all gone crazy! You want somebody in charge? I'm in charge. Because I'm the apex predator of this little group. I am mean and bloodthirsty and wild, and what I say, goes! And I say, you're all bad. Marion, Chester is not going to be your mother. Just forget it. And Chester? I'm sorry, but that's not your baby.

CHESTER: But I love this baby.

GWO GWO: The baby is the problem! Before the baby, you were a good crocodile! *(To Marion.)* And you were a good panda! And I was…well, never mind what I was, but I'm telling you now, this baby's going back!

(Gwo Gwo grabs the baby.)

CHESTER: Back?

GWO GWO: Back to the lab!

CHESTER: No!

MARION: You can't!

GWO GWO: Yes, I can, because I'm the meanest –

MARION: You give that baby back to Chester!

GWO GWO: No!

(They wrestle for the baby.)

CHESTER: Don't hurt the baby!

(Chester dives in. The three of them wrestle until...)

(Rip!)

(The baby is torn to pieces.)

(They stop wrestling.)

CHESTER: No. No, no, no...*(He tries to put the baby back together.)* It's okay, shhh, shhhh, please...

(Beat. No use.)

MARION: We killed it.

(Beat.)

CHESTER: Oh, baby! Baby... *(Cries.)*

GWO GWO: Oh, Chester. Are you crying? Chester...

(Shares a look with Marion. She approaches Chester.)

MARION: There, there, Chester. Shhh. Put your head in my lap. *(She rocks him.)* Shhh. It's okay. Mama's here now.

(Gwo Gwo spies something.)

GWO GWO: Wait a minute. Look at that.

MARION: What?

GWO GWO: Were's the...guts? Look. It's not... Look.

CHESTER: What is it?

GWO GWO: It's... *(Spots his ball.)* It's a toy. *(Picks up his ball, sets it with the baby.)* They're both toys.

MARION: Toys?

GWO GWO: It's a doll. Look.

MARION: You mean, I didn't have a baby? That's not a real baby? And I didn't notice?

GWO GWO: Well, you're a very bad panda, Marion. It's not your fault.

MARION: A toy...

(Chester quite suddenly throws a tantrum. He kicks, he stomps around, he shakes his fists at the sky.)

CHESTER: *(To the heavens.)* Why haven't you ever given me a toy? You give the pandas toys! Maybe Chester would like a toy sometime! *(He collapses on a rock, exhausted.)*

GWO GWO: Oh, Chester. It's okay. I've never killed something before. I don't care for it. Do you?

(Chester shakes his head roughly.)

GWO GWO: I don't want to be a predator anymore. Do you?

(Chester shakes his head.)

GWO GWO: Okay then. *(Kisses him on the top of the head.)* We won't do it anymore. No more predators. We'll be something else.

CHESTER: I want to be a panda. Like you.

GWO GWO: But I'm a bad panda.

CHESTER: I don't mind. I like it.

MARION: But he can't be a panda, Gwo Gwo. He's a crocod-

(Gwo Gwo puts his hand up to silence her. She falls immediately silent.)

GWO GWO: Of course he can be a panda, Marion. Look at him. He's endangered. We're all endangered. We'll be bad pandas together.

MARION: Am I bad panda?

GWO GWO: You're the worst panda in the world.

(They embrace.)

CHESTER: *(Wiping his tears away.)* Of course, on the plus side, that's not a long list.

(They giggle.)

(The television snaps on.)

MARION: Thing! Thing's alive!

GWO GWO: What is that?

MARION: It's a telly-bishin. Chester was telling me earlier.

GWO GWO: What's it do?

CHESTER: It… Different things.

GWO GWO: Look -

MARION: It's talking!

(The static and snow turn to black and silence. They hold their breath expectantly. The picture is grainy and in black and white. On the screen appear two unfamiliar pandas. They grunt and nuzzle each other. All three gasp.)

MARION: Who is that? Pandas!

GWO GWO: Two pandas! Where did they...?

CHESTER: What are they doing?

(Beat.)

GWO GWO: Mating. *(The three stare intently)* So that's how you do it...

(They all instinctively clasp hands. They wordlessly watch the video, transfixed. The video ends. They look at each other in wonderment. Gwo Gwo curls around Chester and starts to giggle. Chester laughs, too. He pulls Marion into the big bear hug. Marion laughs with surprise. The three of them fall into a heap, giddy and laughing and loving each other.)

(Somewhere in the heap, Gwo Gwo and Chester kiss: a promise.)

THE END.

*Also Available From
Original Works Publishing*

<u>**Paper Cranes**</u> **by Kari Bentley-Quinn**

Synopsis: PAPER CRANES is the story of Mona, a recent widow obsessed with the Japanese ritual of folding origami cranes as she grieves the loss of her beloved husband. Mona's teenage daughter, Maddie, is struggling with the demands of her bereft mother and her sexual identity, and begins a romantic relationship with an older woman named Julie. Meanwhile, Julie's best friend, Amy, has begun an intense S&M relationship with a man who is guarding a dark secret. From there, the stories of these five people intertwine, revealing the lasting scars of grief and the desire to be loved.

Cast Size: 1 Male, 4 Females

Lemonade by Mark Krause

Synopsis: Ever hear the one about the struggling comedian and his artist wife who sculpts garbage? All they want is a piece of the American dream. Instead, they're about to lose everything. For the kids' sake they've tried to keep the laughs coming. Will this little family make it? It's going to come down to the final punch line.

Cast Size: 3 Males, 3 Females

Abstract Nude
By Gwydion Suilebhan

Synopsis: "Abstract Nude" is an enigmatic, erotically-charged portrait that seems to reveal more about the people who view it than it reveals about itself. As the painting moves backward in time, it passes from owner to owner, exploding the lives of everyone who encounters it. In one home, the portrait tips the balance in a barely-suppressed power struggle among the members of a well-to-do family. In another, it awakens a great deal of confusion – and passion – between two former fraternity brothers. In the home of the portrait's subject, it inspires nothing but unrequited love and alienation between two dear friends. And finally, back in the moment of its creation, where the story both ends and begins, the painting incites a terrible violence… the tragedy that haunts it wherever it travels, and that cannot be escaped.

Cast Size: 4 Males, 3 Females

Poona the Fuckdog by Jeff Goode

Synopsis: Once upon a time there was a Fuck Dog. Named Poona. Poona was a very lonely Fuck Dog until one day she was visited by her Fairy God Phallus and taught how to play a fun game in her big pink box. Poona suddenly becomes a very popular Fuck Dog! Poona's adventures take her to the Kingdom of Do (where nobody did) ruled by a powerful television set. She meets, among others, Suzy-Suzy Cyber Assassin, a thespian shrub, lost space aliens, and she even talks to God! Poona finally grows old and must tell her fabulous story to all you little kiddies.

Cast Size: cast of 8-17, depending on doubling

The Arctic Circle (and a recipe for Swedish pancakes)
By Samantha Macher

Synopsis: A Brechtian comedy about a woman in a troubled marriage who travels through time, space and Sweden to reexamine her past relationships for solutions to her newly found troubles. Unable to get the clear answers she needs, she must look inside herself to find what she is looking for.

Cast Size: 3 Males, 2 Females

The Why Overhead
By Adam Szymkowicz

Synopsis: At the call center, all are desperate to connect with each other, seek greater meaning and take their desires to extremes. Sam is in love with Violet, a customer who called once with a warranty question, and he smashes all barriers to rendezvous with her. Alan and Sid are blinded in their rivalry for Jessica and together, build a decorative glass window over her cubicle to worship her under. Annie and Nigel have a hate-hate relationship and are each plotting the other's demise. Karen, the department head, plays hooky and makes plans with her sometimes talkative dog to leave the working world entirely in favor of the hobo life. Donald is home too, plotting revenge for being canned as office manager. In the end, the CEO, Mr. Henderson, will sweep in and make everything right, because that's what CEO's do, right?

Cast Size: 7 Males, 5 Females

King Cat Calico Finally Flies Free by Aaron Henne
Synopsis: Heidi Hendrickson is obsessed - she has 150 cats in her eleven hundred square foot apartment, including sixty dead ones in the Frigidaire. She has an especially intimate relationship with the alpha cat, one King Cat Calico, who keeps trying to escape this hellish, tuna tainted, feces stained prison, to no avail. A fun filled exploration of loneliness, possession, and the need to claim one's place in this uncertain world. Featuring a cameo by Rush Limbaugh, singing (literally) the praises of Oxy-Contin, or what he lovingly refers to as his 'little blues.'
Cast Size: 11-16 M/F, Double Casting

Mitzi's Abortion by Elizabeth Heffron

Synopsis: With humor, intelligence and honesty, *Mitzi's Abortion* explores the questions that have shaped the national debate over abortion, and reminds us that whatever we may think we believe, some decisions are neither easy nor simple when they become ours to make. A generous and compassionate comedy with serious themes about a young woman trying to make an intensely personal decision in a system determined to make it a political one.

Cast Size: 4 Males, 3 Female

Nurture by Johnna Adams

Synopsis: Doug and Cheryl are horrible single parents drawn together by their equally horrible daughters. The star-crossed parental units journey from first meeting to first date, to first time, to first joint parent-teacher meeting, to proposal and more. They attempt to form a modern nuclear family while living in perpetual fear of the fruit of their loins and someone abducting young girls in their town.

Cast Size: 1 Male, 1 Female

NOTES

NOTES

NOTES

NOTES

www.ingramcontent.com/pod-product-compliance
Lightning Source LLC
Chambersburg PA
CBHW071725040426
42446CB00011B/2224